WHAT IS MESME[RISM]

AND WHAT ITS CONCOMITANTS

CLAIRVOYANCE AND NECROMANCY?

Second Edition, enlarged.

LONDON:

BOSWORTH & HARRISON, 215 REGENT STREET.

1852.

LONDON
PRINTED BY SPOTTISWOODE AND CO.
NEW-STREET SQUARE

INTRODUCTION.

THE first edition of this pamphlet was printed several years ago. Lately, the sudden outbreak of necromancy in this country has taken such form, that it is thought right to publish a second edition, with some additional observations.

The author has been informed that Dr. Maitland, in his book on this subject, has adopted the same line of argument. The author is glad that he has not seen Dr. Maitland's book, as thus his testimony against these evil practices is independent of any other; and it is a satisfaction to him to know that such a person as Dr. Maitland supports him in his views of these occurrences.

WHAT IS MESMERISM?

And what its Concomitants, Clairvoyance and Necromancy?

———————

THE whole atmosphere of educated society is filled
with this subject. In every company the conversation
turns upon it, and it infects the air around us. Some
are sceptical; some are frightened; some despise the
whole thing, and assert it to be all imposture; some play
with it as an amusement; some seek to the clairvoyant or
to the dead to remove their anxieties and gratify their
curiosity; some receive and yield themselves to the influence of the mesmeriser, or to the guidance of the spirits
professed to be invoked. Some regard it as a mere subject of philosophical inquiry, and assert that they can
explain it all on scientific principles.

But be the various opinions of men what they may, let
us look a little closer into this matter.

There are certain facts before us. There is such a
power as mesmerism; there is such a thing as clairvoyance. Table-moving, &c., is practised. There are certain
individuals who profess to summon the spirits of the
dead, and to give answers by them.

Is there any danger in men practising these occult
arts, and in yielding themselves to them?

Why is it that the Scriptures of truth warn us against
witchcraft, divination, dealing with familiar spirits, and
with the spirits of the dead,—forbid that among the people
of God there should be any that do such things,—number
these among the works which exclude from the kingdom

of heaven, which bring down the plagues of God, and whose end is the lake of fire,—if no such sins can exist, and there be therefore no possibility of committing them? Common sense will tell us that these things must have a reality, and that they can be committed as much as idolatry or adultery, or any other against which the Word of God directs its threatenings. 'There shall not be found among you . . . any that useth divination, or an observer of times, or an enchanter, or a witch, or a charmer, or a consulter with familiar spirits, or a wizard, or a necromancer. For all who do these things are an abomination unto the Lord' (Deut. xviii. 10—12). 'Now the works of the flesh are manifest, . . . idolatry, witchcraft . . . and they which do such things shall not inherit the kingdom of God' (Gal. v. 19—21). 'And the rest of the men which were not killed by these plagues yet repented not of the works of their hands . . . nor of their sorceries' (Rev. ix. 20, 21). 'And . . . sorcerers shall have their part in the lake that burneth with fire' (Rev. xxi. 8).

Let us inquire, very shortly, into the meaning of these words in Deut. xviii. By superficial readers it is supposed that they are merely so many synonymous terms for the same thing. But there is no tautology in Scripture. Each of these terms has its own meaning; and while they all come under one category of sin, yet they are various ramifications of it, and the different readings of the Hebrew, the Septuagint, and the Vulgate, help to throw light upon them.

The Hebrew—A diviner of divinations; a cloud-monger, one who predicts by the appearance of the heavenly bodies, and the clouds; one who predicts by the flight of birds, or the entrails of beasts, or similar signs; one who uses drugs, perfumes, or any other substance, to cast a spell over another; a charmer, or user of cabalistic words to enchant; one who consults an evil spirit, either in himself or in another; a wizard, one who pretends to know, and to be able to reveal, secrets and events; one who seeks to the spirits of the dead for information on any point.

The Septuagint — Predicting predictions; seeking omens or voices; divining by birds; using drugs; chanting an incantation; having a demon, or speaking out of the belly; observing prodigies; questioning the dead.

The Vulgate — He who inquires of a soothsayer; observes dreams and auguries; a witch; an enchanter; one who consults Python; one who seeks the truth from the dead.

Which may be classed as follows :—

1. Foretellers of facts, or revealers of what would be otherwise hidden from men; *seers*, and that not from any *resident* insight.

2. Observers of times as affecting destiny.

3. Observers of signs in heaven or in earth.

4. Casters of a spell upon living men, constraining or enabling them to act and speak when under the influence of that spell.

5. Binders of other bodily creatures, of spirits, of devils, or of inanimate matter, constraining them or causing them to speak or act.

6. Binders of the spirits of the departed by a spell, or of those pretending to be the spirits of the dead, to act or speak.

7. Those who have supernatural or preternatural insight or wisdom from evil spirits dwelling in them, as oracles, &c.

8. Those who draw their insight or wisdom from consulting the departed, or evil spirits, pretending to be the spirits of the departed.

Thus we see that these terms in Deuteronomy are not mere synonymes, but various modes of that evil working which in the New Testament are summed up in the one word φαρμακεία, witchcraft, rendered in the Vulgate by maleficium, or veneficium, because it is most wicked, hurtful, and poisonous to the spirits of those who use it, or upon whom it is used; and it is called in Gal. v. one of the works of the flesh, and classed with idolatry, because it is having recourse to the evil spirit instead of to God, and also because it is the prying of the flesh into things hidden from the powers of the natural understanding, through the means of magic and evil, instead of applying to God for such revelation, if it be necessary or good to have such disclosures made. And indeed while all these terms above used indicate, as we have said, various modifications of unlawful practice, they all have reference to that class of sin which may be defined as — first, the inquiring into any secret or hidden thing, past, present, or future, by consulting any person or being, or through any substance, or any means whatsoever, in the air, or earth, or hell, by divination, signs, auguries, visions, or dreams; the seeking to familiar spirits, or to the dead, or to any one, or by the means of any one who claims either really or falsely to have the power of answering, whether by himself or by others. Secondly, the using of any spell, charm, enchantment, or any substance ponderable or imponderable on the spirit, mind, or body, or persons of others, living or dead, devils or men, whereby to cause them to give replies to such inquiries. Having thus far cleared our ground, surely it will not require much consideration to come to the conclusion that mesmerism, clairvoyance, electro-biology, and such like, and more especially 'necromancy,' or consulting and conversing with the spirits of the dead, or devils professing and pretending to be such, are manifestly comprised under the things thus prohibited.

It may be as well to point out here to those who have not reflected on the subject, that the word necromancy does not mean conjuring, in the commonly used sense of the word. The word 'Doresh el hamethim' and νεκρομαντεία, means seeking to the departed for information, holding dialogues with them, they speaking to the living.

One of the besetting sins among baptised men in these days is ignorance of, or scepticism in regard to, spiritual things — We do not mean doctrinal, but spiritual existences and operations.

There are three leavens we are bidden to beware of — that of the Pharisee, that of the Herodian, and that of the Sadducee.

The first — Hypocrisy — pretending to have faith.

having none ; professing and following Church forms and doctrines, whether High Church or Low, without receiving the life of God through them, and walking in the power of it.

Second — the Herodian — not seeking to please God alone in Church matters, but the powers that be ; not caring whether 'the Church be governed in the right way' or not, provided that the earthly ruler gives peace and prosperity.

Thirdly — the leaven of the Sadducee, which consists in 'not believing in the resurrection of the body, nor in angels, nor in spirits.'

That these three leavens have leavened Christendom, it is not needful here to enter into any argument to prove.

Leaving the other two, it is to the consideration of the third we would at present address ourselves.

There are spirits. We will not argue about it. We dogmatise.

There are spirits. There is the Holy Ghost, the Holy Spirit of God, present with and dwelling with those who receive and honour Him, and yield to Him — grieved and resisted by those who refuse to be guided by Him. There are angels, servants of God fulfilling His will, ministering spirits sent forth to minister to the heirs of salvation. There is Satan, that evil spirit, who resisteth God, and teaches others to do the same. There are demons, evil spirits, the angels of Satan, the deceivers, tempters, seducers, and befoolers of men.

It is of no importance here to enter into the question of who or what Satan was and is, nor who or what are the δαιμόνια of Scripture, except to assert that they are persons.

These, both the good and the evil, are not emanations, influences, nor abstract principles, good or evil, but are entities, beings, persons. The Holy Ghost is not an emanation or influence, but the Third Person in the Most Holy Trinity. Angels are persons, each with his own separate existence, will, and faculties. So is Satan, 'the prince of the power of the air.' So are demons.

We will not argue the matter. Those who are deluded by the Sadducean leaven into disbelieving this will some day find it true, and that with one or other they will have to associate for ever.

But there is a modified form of Sadduceeism we have need to warn men against,—viz..that while they believe, or think they believe, in the abstract proposition that there are angels and devils, yet they cannot bring themselves to believe that these have in this our day any power to act.

The two great divisions of the Church, the Roman and the Protestant, err in two opposite forms in this matter. The Roman has always professed to believe in, and to recognise, the actings of spiritual beings, good and evil ; miracles and gifts of the Holy Ghost ; visions and prophesyings ; ministrations of angels ; workings of, and possessions by, evil spirits ; but through departing from the truth in doctrine, she has lost the true discernment, διάκρισις, between good and evil spirits or powers, and so receives things as from God which are too often from the evil one, and lays herself open to agencies and revelations which have led into error and deception on very important points.

On the other hand, a vast majority of the members of the Protestant Churches have come well nigh to disbelieve and deny the possibility of any *present* spiritual manifestation or working at all. They talk of the Holy Ghost as if He were a mere influence, and not a Holy and Divine person, present with the Church. They will tell you that it was never intended that He should work or manifest Himself as in days of old ; they exclude from their thoughts the idea of angels ever helping them in any way ; and as to devils, while they retain some vague notion of Satan tempting men, they assert that there are no such things now as familiar spirits, possession by evil spirits, or demoniacs. Many contend that Satan was bound when Christ ascended into heaven, so that he can neither possess men nor work in and by them now, as he did in ancient times ; and in regard to witchcraft, sorcery, &c., they maintain that it is all very well for the dark ages to put credence in such nonsense, but it is unworthy of these days of education and science. Nay, almost every modern Protestant Church History coolly informs us that all spiritual working and power ceased with the lives of the apostles and their contemporaries.

It is true such men find it difficult to maintain their theory. If you ask them when the power of Satan was contracted and limited in these things, they will answer, ‘When our Lord rose and ascended, and led captivity captive;’ and they quote the text—‘I saw Satan fall like lightning from heaven,’ which, even if it did refer to our Lord’s time, and was not spoken prophetically, would not apply, for it does not say, ‘I saw Satan cast out of the earth.’ And chap. xii. of Revelation shows us that whenever the time does come for Satan to be cast out of the heavenly places, his power and wrath on the earth will then be manifested even more than ever. And when you point out to them that *after* our Lord’s ascension, Philip the Evangelist cast out unclean spirits (Acts viii. 7), and Peter (Acts v. 16), and Paul (Acts xix. 12), and that the sons of Sceva tried to do the same and could not, but the evil spirit prevailed against them, and tore and wounded them (Acts xix. 13), and that Simon Magus and Elymas practised sorcery (Acts viii. 9, xiii. 8); when they are thus beaten out of their position by Scripture itself, then they shift their ground, and say that these manifestations, both of good and evil power, ceased when the apostles and their contemporaries died. And when you bring against this notion also undisputed Church history, and quote passage after passage from Justin Martyr, Irenæus, Tertullian, Cyprian, Theophilus, Lactantius, &c., for generations after the apostles, distinctly asserting in their day, on the one hand, the existence and manifestation of the power of the Holy Ghost among them; and on the other, not only the possession of men by evil spirits, but also the casting out and silencing of the same by the ministers of the churches, and challenging the Jew and the heathen to come into the churches and witness this for themselves; then they endeavour to select some other epoch on grounds as easy to be refuted as the previous ones—such as the conversion of Constantine, the decree of Theodosius, &c.; although the very fact of the existence and continuance of the office of Exorcist long after either of those periods, and of all the canons against the use of witchcraft, show that the Church entertained no such opinion, but held that evil spirits could still work, and possess men, and still by the power of God be cast out. And Scripture gives not the slightest ground for supposing that the power of Satan and his angels is in the least degree curtailed. If men, in going through a lunatic asylum, cannot distinguish between the lunatic and the demoniac, it is because the leaven of the Sadducee has eaten out the spirit of discernment in them. St. Paul tells us 'To put on the whole armour of God, that we may be able to stand against the wiles of the devil. For we wrestle not against flesh and blood, but against principalities, against powers, against the rulers of the darkness of this world, against wicked spirits in heavenly places (*margin*).' St. Peter, 'To be sober, vigilant; because our adversary the devil, as a roaring lion, walketh about seeking whom he may devour.' And St. John, in his first epistle, warns us 'Not to believe every spirit, but to try them whether they be of God or not;' and in the Revelation foretells all the evil Satan is to do on the earth till the time of his final doom come. No; by the coming of our Lord and His victory over Satan, and by all He has done, and is doing, for us, there is a power given to us whereby we also can obtain the victory over him and baffle all his wiles; but the devil's power is not diminished, though doubtless baptised men are guarded from it in a way heathen are not, unless they willfully put themselves under him; and the erroneous ideas of modern days on this head can easily be accounted for, when we see how men have confounded the power that was given to the Church to fight against and overcome devils, and to cast them out of men, with that predicted, and still future, binding of Satan, which remains to be fulfilled at the second coming of our Lord.

This, then, is really the state of things in the Church at present—either, on the one hand, gross superstition and undiscerning admission of impostures, and the working of evil spirits; or, on the other, sceptical and scornful unbelief in, and practical opposition to, the idea of any spiritual working and manifestation at all, whether good or evil.

Men in the latter state take refuge, as an excuse for their unbelief, in the many cases of superstitious folly of individuals, and of impostures by priests, both pagan and Christian, and others, recorded in all ages; and in the various instances of detected deception, or decided failure in the pretensions of mesmerists, clairvoyants, mediums, &c., in the present day. But it has ever been so. Wherever there has been any working of evil spirits, anything of magic in any shape, there falsehood and imposture or self-delusion have also been present. The oracles of the heathen were half imposture, half the real power of the Pythonic spirit; and whoever will yield himself to be an instrument of false and lying spirits, will become himself false and lying, and self-deceived; and he will always be ready to eke out an answer from his own mind if the spiritual power be not present to give it. God has so ordered it that there will be always sufficient to prove to any honest mind, by exposures of this sort, that the work is not of Him, and the instruments used not His servants.

But, in spite of all the numerous instances of fraud, superstition, imposture, or failure, that may be easily adduced in this, and in every age, there is, after all, such a thing as the real existence of spiritual personalities and powers—there are, we repeat, the operations of the blessed Spirit of God; there are the operations of angels; there are the operations of devils; there are such things as magic, and divination, and witchcraft, and necromancy, and familiar spirits, and curious, occult, unlawful arts, of which God condemns and prohibits the use under the most terrible penalties.

Now, of late years, there have risen up amongst us men using, or rather reviving the use of, a curious art, which is denominated mesmerism, from a Swiss physician, who practised it in the end of the eighteenth century, although it can be traced back to the remotest ages. And it is a serious question, seeing how prevalent the practice of it is becoming,— May we use this art or not? Is it a mere physical operation, like the use of laudanum, or of electricity, or galvanism? or, Is it a spiritual operation? or, Is it both physical and spiritual combined? and if the last, Is the spirit that is called into exercise good or evil? or, May it be either good or evil, according as the operator wills?

We shall not take up time by going into the numerous and incontrovertible evidences that mesmerism is a fact—a reality, and not a trick or imposture, nor the mere creature of a deluded or excited imagination. It would swell this pamphlet beyond the purpose for which it is written; neither will we relate the instances which prove that clairvoyance is a reality; so also table-moving without the contact of any human being; and also the communications of spirits professing to be the souls of the departed.

We mention one of each merely as a specimen. One lady we know personally is very easily thrown into the mesmeric trance, and immediately becomes clairvoyante. The first time she was so, inquiries were made of her in regard to the son of a lady present who had not been heard of for some time, and about whom his mother was under great anxiety; and Mrs —— described exactly where he was and what he was doing, which proved afterwards to have been the case on that day. And this sort of thing continually occurs.

TABLE-MOVING. Faraday has convinced all scientific men that table-moving is a mere mechanical and physical muscular action, although perhaps involuntary on the part of the operators. But a friend of ours, a clergyman, as the thing was prevailing in his parish, determined to prove it for himself. He made his wife and children and servants stand behind him in the corner of his dining-room, so that all were several feet from the dining-table in the centre of the room. He bid the table 'Go into the opposite corner.' It did so. 'Stand up on one leg.' It did so. 'Throw that book off.' The book was flung up into the air as by a hand. He said to us, 'From that time I was convinced of the reality of such a thing, and also that it was evil, and I ever after warned all my parishioners against it.' Where was Faraday's muscular action here?

SPIRIT-COMMUNICATIONS AND RAPPINGS, ETC.—Various instances have come to our knowledge lately, where persons who have gone to those *séances*, have been followed in their own homes for several days after by the greatest annoyances, by the continual rappings on the walls and other parts of their rooms, till, perfectly terror-struck, they have prayed vehemently to be delivered.

But we purposely abstain from relating the numberless instances continually brought under our notice of the horrible reality of the presence of evil spirits in these transactions, for we do not wish to stain the minds and spirits of our readers by doing so; but we do wish to prevent any from meddling with these things, and to convince them that they are not matters to make a plaything of, and that it is neither lawful nor innocent to practise such, nor to have recourse to those that do.

People may perhaps ask, 'Why do you include mesmerism in the list of unlawful things? Surely there is an innocent use of that power?'

That is just the question. First, Is mesmerism a mere natural and physical operation? Secondly, Has it not led on to all these other phenomena which we are denouncing?

One way in which men vindicate the use of this occult art, is by alleging that the power brought into exercise is an invisible imponderable natural substance which fills creation, and is identical with electricity or the magnetic fluid, which modern discovery asserts to be one. Granting this, we have but the more reason for serious reflection, when we consider that it may only facilitate the working of invisible spirits; for, however men may dispute it, it is a fact, that the material creature is used by God Himself, and also by Satan, as an instrument and means of spiritual operation on man. God uses men, the word of men, the laying on of the hands of men, water, bread, wine, oil, as means whereby He works various and manifold grace in and upon men. So does Satan also use the material creature to work his evil purposes on men, perhaps to a much greater extent than we have any idea of; and in all witchcraft and sorcery there is the use of cabalistic words — words of incantation, songs, &c.,—or the intervention of some substance, ponderable or imponderable, in charms, amulets, crystals, iron beds, perfumes, &c., &c. Nay, the very name in the New Testament, φαρμακεία, indicates the use of natural substance and means in some shape. As in holy things there are the acting of man as God's minister, the use of the natural substance, and the operation of the Spirit; so in all sorcery there are the acting of the man as Satan's minister, the use of the natural substance, and the operation of the evil spirit.

Therefore, admitting that in mesmerism there is an imponderable substance, a 'magnale magnum,'—call it magnetic or what you will,—brought into exercise, we affirm that herein consists the greater danger, as it is by this that the invisible spirit works. And thus, as the practice of mesmerism progresses, we find, as detailed in Gregory's book on this subject, that coins, ink, medicines, &c., are now used to convey the mesmeric influence from one person to another.

We maintain that no properties of any mere natural substance, visible or invisible, ponderable or imponderable, are capable of explaining and accounting for the effects produced by mesmerism, and that there is more than sufficient evidence to demonstrate that there is spiritual and preternatural action also, and that such spiritual action is evil. Some indeed hold that there is no magnetic or other imponderable substance, but that the spirit of the operator goes forth from him by an exercise of his will to work upon the other. But this in no way obviates the charge; for if even this were possible, such an exercise of a man's spirit over that of another would be unquestionably wicked, as we will prove by and by. Some also say, that in cases of mesmeric healing, it is only the superabundance of electricity and animal heat, health, and strength, that goes out of one stronger man's body into that of a weaker. But how does this account for the casting into the trance, the accompanying clairvoyance, which the operator probably does not possess himself, the submission of the patient's will, &c.?

We believe that there is a material, imponderable, subtle, substance called into action, and therefore, that this very thing is more helpful to the sin of witchcraft, because the evil spirit uses both the mesmeriser as his minister (ignorantly and unconsciously it may be), and the imponderable substance also, to operate his purpose.

The phenomena which accompany mesmerism, if investigated, will show that there is not only some imponderable substance employed, but also a spiritual and preternatural power, acting not only on the bodily senses, but also on the spirit, and mind, and will of the mesmerised ; and that these phenomena are not those of the presence and operation of the Spirit of God, but of the presence of an inferior, miserable, and evil spirit, whose revelations and answers to questions, where mesmerism is followed by clairvoyance, like those of the pythonesses and diviners of old, are as often wrong as right, as often failures as true disclosures, and often also enigmatical, obscure, seductive and lying, and often feigned.

Indeed, mesmerisers who are not yet poisoned with the philosophical leaven of the neologist, will sometimes confess there is a twofold operation — physical and spiritual — natural and preternatural — combined. One, an eminent medical man, who practises mesmerism, and mesmerised his medicines, and yet is a good, well-intentioned, religious man too, admitted this to us; but alleged, that whether it was a good or evil spirit that was used depended on the will of the operator, and that he himself always used the good. The fallacy of this we shall see as we proceed.

Let us now examine a little the evidences that there is something preternatural and supernatural — both the laying aside of the natural faculties of man, and the going beyond and above the natural faculties of man, in mesmerism.

In the use of the mere natural creature — medicine,

galvanism, &c.,— you may cure disease, you may cast into a deep sleep; yet you cannot make the man, in that state, think, speak, and act. Whereas, in mesmerism you not only cast into a deep sleep, but you give power to the sleeping one to think, speak, and act. You can make a man see, his eyes being shut; hear, his ear deaf to all outward impression; speak from his stomach or his tongue; and can when you please, by a little additional process, make him use all the members of his body to do what *you* will, wholly irrespective of *his own will.* And moreover, this is generally accompanied by a greater or less degree of clairvoyance, during which persons can read the thoughts of others, describe places which they never saw, give account of events entirely beyond the compass of their own knowledge, divine secrets, and give replies in answer to inquiries on things hidden. If these things are not preternatural and supernatural, what is? If this does not come under what is prohibited in Deuteronomy, what does? It is divination.

Again, you cure disease by medicine, or by the galvanic battery, yet these cast no spell on the man; these defile not, oppress not, the spirit of the man operated upon. But in mesmerism you cast a spell over the man, and over his spirit. For the time he is absolutely under the control of the operator. But the thing does not stop here. It is a well-known feature in mesmerism that, after a course of it, the will and spirit of the person on whom it is practised become, in an extraordinary manner, abjectly and permanently subservient to the control and will of the mesmeriser, not only while in the trance, but during waking hours. Yes; there has been a *spell* at work, some *spiritual* influence which does not accompany the use of medicine, nor of mere natural magnetism or electricity. A friend of ours went to one of the celebrated hydropathic establishments, and, the water-cure not succeeding, the physician of the place recommended him to be mesmerised; but he added, 'Do not let your *servant* do it.' That meant, 'If you allow your servant to do it, he will obtain an improper influence over you; he will command you and not you him.' And that doctor is a mesmeriser of long standing, and of repute as a physician.

It is attempted to be said, that this is only the influence of a man with a strong mind and will over one that is weaker. But they who are in the habit of observing these things, will easily discern the different features that accompany the mere natural influence of one man's mind and spirit over another's, and that which is permanently obtained by the spell of the mesmeriser over his prostrated victim. If this does not come under what is prohibited in Deuteronomy, what does?

Some endeavour to get rid of all this by saying, 'We are not to pronounce things to be supernatural and evil because they are new, or because we cannot explain the principles of them, as yet incomprehensible to us ; for who can say what science may discover ? and if some newly disclosed, some sixth sense, as we have heard it called, is about to be developed in these days, what right have we to assume that its exercise is supernatural and evil ? But this is false reasoning ; for, first, Scripture does not permit it to be said, because you cannot explain the principle on which, or comprehend how, perfumes, charms, or spells, constrain the spirit of a man or a devil to answer your questions, therefore you may doubt whether the thing is beyond the natural powers of man, and the practice evil. And secondly, it is false because this is no new thing, no new faculty now first brought to light, that a man can be thrown into a trance, and then made to see, speak, and act ; or that men heal diseases by charms, magic, and enchantments, and occult practices. Such things are as old as the oldest records, sacred or profane ; and they have always been treated in such records as supernatural. Thirdly, it is false, for there is no bringing in of a sixth sense in aid of the other five, but a substitution of something in the room of the five which God has given, making a man to see, to hear, to feel, to taste, to act, and speak, while every faculty of the body, eye, ear, nose, touch, and tongue, are closed in overpowering sleep, the conscience and the will being at the same time in utter abeyance also.

It is the annihilation of the *man*, as to all his senses, and above all, as to his conscience and *will*, the noblest part of man — that especially wherein he is made in the image of God — the highest gift of God to him as a creature, that inviolable gift which God Himself will not meddle with, but always leaves in its integrity. It is a shameful condition into which no man has a right to allow himself to be brought, that he is compelled to use the members of his body and the faculties of his mind at the will of another man, while his own conscience and his own will are rendered incapable of being exercised. One of the magazines which report the cases of healing by mesmerism, says, 'As to the subjection of the will during the sleep, we fully admit the fact, and regard it as one of our most curious phenomena ; and where is the harm of it if it be properly exercised by judicious mesmerisers ? That this power might be abused, like every other power and every other gift, we do not deny ; the evil-disposed may do what is evil with that which is alone excellent and good. . . . . Even if there were any mischief, would it be enough to counterbalance the immense amount of benefit received in the matter of health ?'

But without reference to any practical evil results that might, and have occurred, we say that the thing itself is abstractedly and essentially evil and wicked, and not to be made a plaything of. It is sin to suspend the will and conscience of a responsible creature, and yet give him the power of action, and that entirely under the will and control of another creature, to do good or to do evil as *he* will. For instance, if divination be a sin, and it be denounced as such in the Scriptures, and a man or woman in the mesmeric trance is made by the will of the mesmeriser to 'divine,' then both are committing deadly sin — the one who wills and the one who yields his or her will thus to the other.

We repeat it is in itself, even suppose no clairvoyance or other acts follow, essentially and abstractedly evil to put oneself in such a position. It is what God Himself not only does not require, but will not have from us, even towards Himself. God has created us with a 'will,' otherwise we should not be responsible beings ; and He will not permit us to forego that responsibility by voluntarily casting our will into temporary suspension, and acting by the will of another, without the power of resistance. God indeed requires us to subject our will unto His will, and also, when lawfully required, to the will of those whom He has set over us; but He will not have our will annihilated, or the action of it suspended for a moment, so that we should become mere machines, even in His hand — how much less in the hand of any creature! Every act of ours in doing the will of God, or even in the exercise of supernatural spiritual functions, such as those described in 1 Cor. xiv., must be a conscious willing act, a personal self-direction of the man at the time. It is the great distinction between the operation and acts of the Holy Ghost and those of satanic possession, that the devil *possesses* the man and forces him to acts of violence, while the Spirit of God acts by the free will of the man. God has given us a free will, and we must not allow it to be merged in the will of any other creature whatsoever. And we may be assured of this, that if the devil has got possession of any man so as to force him to deeds of violence and sin, the man must have first yielded to temptation and to the enemy before ever he could have obtained such a possession.

God commands us, indeed, to obey those who have the rule over us, and to bring our will into *subordination* to them, in church, and state, and family. Would that the good old rule in the catechism were indeed learned by heart and practised from the heart. ' My duty towards my neighbour . . . To love, honour, and succour my father and mother. To honour and obey the king, and all that are put in authority under him. To submit myself to all my governors, teachers, spiritual pastors and masters. To order myself lowly and reverently to all my betters.'

The evil of the times we live in is that which St. Paul speaks of, ' This know also, that in the last days perilous times shall come. For men shall be lovers of their own selves . . . disobedient to parents . . . heady, high-minded,' &c. (2 Tim iii.). But while God would have us subordinate, and 'with willing wills be willingly ruled,' yet He would have us ever to keep possession of our wills so that we may be free to act contrary to all men's wills if they require us to do something contrary to the plain will and law of God, as we see exemplified in the cases of Shadrach, Meshach, and Abednego, Daniel, Peter, and John, &c.

To have our will ruled is one thing, and is lawful and right, and to be unruly is sin ; but to have it suspended, abrogated, is quite another thing, and is unlawful and wrong. And it is unlawful and wrong, and a shame, even where the will is not suspended, to allow any human being to obtain over us that permanently morbid and undue influence which is confessedly done by the mesmerisers over the mesmerised after a certain time.

What is the great error and sin of the Jesuit system ? Is it not their doctrine that you are to abnegate and make void your will, and be in the hand of your superior like the staff in the hand of an old man ? Yet the Jesuit sin is, after all, rather the mere disregard of man's personal judgement and conscience as to good and evil. Whereas the sin of mesmerism exceeds this by annihilating *pro tempore* the will and conscience altogether. Another man may make you do what *he* wills, the most benevolent actions, or the most cruel, fierce, and murderous ; the most prostrate acts of reverence and worship, or those of the utmost scorn, contempt, profanity, and intolerable vanity ; the most righteous deeds, or the most open and unscrupulous dishonesty or uncleanness. We knew a man who constantly amused himself by getting people into his house and setting a mesmeric doctor to lay his hand on the various organs of their heads while in a trance, and by this means cause them to perform all manner of strange and fantastic actings of reverence, prayer, wrath, pride, vanity, theft, &c. ; and yet he meant no evil, nor did he think that he was doing any, nor how he was degrading human nature in the objects of his experiments. Yes ; a man may make another who will submit to this occult power do all these things, besides bringing him under the continuous bad influence which remains when the mesmeric trance is passed. And it is no argument to say 'that no respectable physician or other person will ever use this power and influence to an improper end.' That is not the question; the thing is sin in itself, without regard to any consequences, good or bad: besides, how do we know what a man may please, or the devil tempt him to do?

It may be said, 'If you allege that the mere act of throwing a man into a trance, and then making him see, hear, speak, and act at the will of another, his own being in abeyance, is in the abstract evil, how does it accord with the fact that God Himself has done this, as is frequently recorded in Scripture?'

This is a mistake. God has never done so. Nowhere in Scripture do we find an instance of a man's conscience and will being suspended. We find that while God gave to men to speak in prophecy, or in spiritual trance, to see and hear, speak and act, it was never without their will and conscience being awake and in exercise at the time. The integrity of the responsible being was preserved entire, and they could reason and do what they willed. Solomon (2 Sam. iii.) could choose what to ask, and was rewarded for *willing* to choose what was pleasing to God. John (Rev. x.) was going to write what he heard the seven thunders utter, and was forbidden. He was going to fall down and worship the angel (Rev. xix.), and was told not to do so; and he exercised his will and conscience in obeying. In prophesying the spirits of the prophets are subject to the prophets, and they could refrain from speaking if they *would* (1 Cor. xiv. 32). In no case recorded in Scripture did the man act as an irresponsible being.

Now, no one doubts that when in the Bible a man is described as seeing, speaking, and acting while in a trance, he is under supernatural influence, good or evil. The fact of his so acting was held to be sufficient evidence of his condition. On what ground, then, do we doubt, when a man is so acting in a mesmeric trance, that his condition is supernatural?

There is one difficulty in dealing with this subject — viz., the fact that many cases of healing occur under mesmeric power; and that even good men, clergy, doctors, &c., use it to that end. But this becomes a difficulty only from not considering the extent of Satan's power and devices, and that in all ages cases of healing are recorded as performed by magic, by charms, by relics, &c.; and now that the last days are to all appearance drawing on, we have reason to expect that the enemy of souls will be more subtle and active than ever. The time is hastening when the controversy between the good and the evil powers must manifest itself in a more open way than has been hitherto seen on the earth, in order to bring out, on one hand, the predicted apostasy, and on the other, the perfecting and saving of those who receive and obey the truth.

Keeping this in view, it will not be difficult to see some of the reasons why Satan should introduce, or rather revive — for they are all old forms of evil — mesmerism, clairvoyance, electro-biology, various modes of divination, and necromancy.

The object is twofold. With some men it familiarises the mind with spiritual things; it takes away that natural awe and dread with which God has surrounded men in dealing with the unseen, and causes them to approach such as familiar things; and so all reverence and holy fear of God and His good angels departs, and the abhorrence of, and resistance to, evil spirits is lost: and *familiarity* with spirits, good or bad, is an abomination in the eyes of God.

It leads to a direct breach of God's commandment not to consult diviners, and more especially not the spirits of the dead. It leads to every species of false doctrine, and denial of what God has made known to us in Holy Scripture. Witness all the blasphemous books and magazines published in England, America, France, and Germany, on this subject; that there are millions of people daily consulting by necromancy the spirits of the dead, or, at least, those professing to be such, and guiding their conduct and their faith by the communications received from them. For the first time now since the world began, the consulting of these familiar spirits is openly advocated and practised as a good and right thing, in the face of day, among the people of God, unreproved, unrepressed, unpunished. Even many of those who censure these practices do so, not on the ground of its being wicked, but on the ground of its unreality. The article in the leading journal the other day, instead of reproving the immorality of these proceedings, was written in a tone of 'badinage,' treating it all as absurd, instead of showing that, whether true or false, reality or imposture, the very professing to do them is wickedness, and is not a matter of 'badinage' at all.

The second object Satan has in introducing these things, is that to another class of minds they strengthen the neology, the infidelity, and the Sadduceeism of the day. Many have already declared that the miracles of our Lord and His apostles were done by mesmeric power; and assert that mesmerism is the gift of healing named in Scripture among the gifts of the Holy Ghost. Has not even a clergyman of the Church of England written that missionaries should learn this art, so that they may be able to heal diseases, as promised in Scripture? One's heart and hand trembles as one writes such things, which are well nigh, if not quite, blasphemy against the Holy Ghost. The blasphemy against Him was saying that what our Lord did by the power of God the Holy Ghost, was done by the spirit of Beelzebub. What is it but blasphemy to say that which devils do is done by the Holy Spirit of God? Or even supposing that it is a mere natural power that is called into exercise, it is well nigh blasphemy to call that a gift of the Holy Ghost, and done by Him, for the creature is not God. Surely men do not reflect when they say such things. Is it not written in Scripture that the gift of healing is one of the supernatural and extraordinary gifts of the Holy Ghost? (1 Cor. xii. 9.) These men assert that mesmerism is a natural gift of creation, a natural power in man; and in the same breath they affirm that this mesmeric power is the gift of healing mentioned in Scripture. Has common sense left them? And if, on the other hand, they declare that this mesmeric power and gift of healing is supernatural, then they condemn themselves, and prove they are acting under evil power, and the power of a familiar spirit; for our God the Holy Ghost, whose name is not to be named but with holy reverence, could never condescend to be used as mesmerisers use their power; nor would He throw people into mesmeric sleep to answer idle questions, to gratify the curiosity, or appease the anxieties of foolish or faithless men. God is not a familiar spirit, and woe be to the man who thinks He is, or endeavours to make Him so. Have reverence, and fear, and common sense, taken their departure, that men can think and say such things?

Again, another motive that Satan has, is not only to throw a slur and contempt on the past workings of God, but also upon any that may yet be done by Him as the last days come on, which Scripture gives us ground to expect; and also upon any putting forth of Divine power to heal in answer to the prayers of His people, and in the use of the ordinances and ministries of His Church.

There are two legitimate ways of healing diseases: one, *natural*, in the use of physicians, and medicines formed of the substances of the earth; the other *supernatural*, according to what is directed in Scripture, through the prayer of God's ministers, through the laying on of their hands, through the use of oil; and this is accompanied with confession of fault, forgiveness of sin, and the saving of the soul as well as of the body. 'Is any man sick among you? let him send for the elders of the church; and let them pray over him, anointing him with oil in the name of the Lord: and the prayer of faith shall save the sick, and the Lord shall raise him up; and if he have committed sins, they shall be forgiven him. Confess your faults one to another, and pray one for another, that ye may be healed' (Jas. v. 14—16).

And what is mesmerism but the mockery of all this — the devil's substitute for it? If the use of medicine succeeds not, send, not for the elders of the Church, the ministers of God, but for a mesmeriser. Receive not the laying on of the hands of Christ's ministers, but the deadly waving of the hands of the mesmeriser. No need to confess faults, or that there should be any prayer for forgiveness, and that thus God's holy love and mercy come out to you, in healing not only the sickness of the body, but the wounds of the soul: but let witchcraft heal the body, and leave the soul and spirit, not even where they were, but worse, with the slimy traces of the track of the serpent that has passed over them, torpid, and weakened, and overmastered.

Surely this is not God's way; it is contrary to His way; it is the denial of His ordinances; it is the substitution of another thing for them, which, as far as we can see, is an ordinance of the devil. It is the base counterfeit of the long-lost true golden coin of the Church. It is the dogs licking the beggar's sores, while that which ought to administer comfort and healing has been withheld.

The Church ought in all ages to have kept the faith of God's good will and power to heal in the use of His ordinances, as St. James directs us. But throughout the length and breadth of Christendom, where is it? The Roman Catholics, while in their 'Rituale' they have retained the true form of the rite, have *practically* turned it into 'Extreme Unction,' to dismiss *from* life, instead of to restore *to* life; although there are numerous instances in every priest's experience wherein God has shown Himself faithful to His own ordinance, and by it has raised up and restored the sick to health, in spite of their perversion of it. The Protestants, on the other hand, have neglected it altogether, alleging that oil was only meant to be used in apostolic days, retaining only a service for the Visitation of the Sick, wherein, for adults, there is not even a decided prayer and request for healing. And in both Roman and Protestant practice, the prayers for the commending the

souls of the dying to God are used at the same time, or
in the same service, which should have been confined to
asking for healing, whereby is betrayed the lack of
faith in the healing ordinance. No wonder, then, that
through the perversion or forgetfulness and omission of
God's way, in the ignorance that exists as to spiritual
matters, both good and evil, and in the contemptuous
unbelief that there can be such a thing as witchcraft,
and that it is one of the forbidden works of the flesh,
Satan should have substituted, and even good men as
well as bad have accepted the remedy proposed by the
powers of darkness, instead of the one provided by God
in His Church. And no wonder if, should it please
God to restore faith to His Church and the use of the
ordinances, and men be healed thus, there will be those
who will say, ' Do we not effect the same thing by our
mesmerism? It is but a natural thing after all.'

There are some who argue that the healing power of
mesmerism may be used separately from any evil, that
they can go so far and there stop; but we deny it. Mesmeric power cannot be used except accompanied by the
phenomena which we have demonstrated to be evil. You
cannot exercise the power of mesmerism without the
accompanying trance, and without the accompanying
influence over the mesmerised, and in too many cases
without the accompanying clairvoyance.

Some also would dispute that mesmerism has anything to do with the other spiritual phenomena — table-
moving and necromancy. But one followed the other.
It began by men claiming to use this magnetic power
and their will over men, and then it proceeded to clairvoyance, and then to moving tables by this same magnetic power, and from table-moving to table-rapping, and
from table-rapping to rappings on the walls, and hands
appearing through the tables, and then to spiritual
mediums and the appearance of spirits to such, and necromancy, or dialogues with the dead, in all the hideous
forms that now stain this metropolis and all other parts
of Christendom.

There are worse evils than even these in the background yet to come ; but even these that have appeared have led the followers of them into all manner of false doctrine and error, and contemptible and profane ideas of that awful subject, 'What is the state of the departed?' and what the all-important distinction between the state of the blessed and that of the wicked, making void the parable of our Lord of the different conditions of Lazarus and Dives (and let it be remembered that 'while our Lord spake parables, He never spake *fables.*' —DEAN TRENCH), and every other part of Scripture that bears upon the subject.

It may perhaps be permitted here to inquire, Are these spirits who thus appear and answer questions really the spirits of the dead, or evil spirits pretending to be them, and assuming their forms ? Lately in Germany one of these spirits pretending to be the spirit of the father of a person present, a clergyman commanded it in the name of the Lord Jesus to confess whether he was the spirit of the person he professed to be, and the answer thus compelled was, 'I am not.' A lady of rank in this country went, not long ago, to one of these places where the persons wishing to consult divination are requested to put their hands on a table, and immediately a power lays hold of their hand and guides it to write the answers to their questions. This lady put her hand on the table, and directly felt the power seize her hand and make her write. At last she got alarmed, and said, 'I command you in the name of the Lord Jesus to say who you are that are using my hand;' and the reply was, 'I am your familiar devil.' It is more than probable, then, looking at what Scripture says about the respective places of separate spirits till the day of the resurrection, that the spirits of the dead cannot roam about in the way these appearances would lead men to believe, but that they are demons who assume their names and forms. And that one reason why the Witch of Endor was so astonished, was that Samuel really personally came up out of Hades at her bidding.

However, be this as it may—be the whole thing imposture and trick and delusion (though this idea is difficult to reconcile with all the accounts that come to us from every quarter of the occurrences that take place on these occasions)—be it devils, or be it the spirits of the departed,—it is wrong, detestable, and wicked from beginning to end, and those that practise these things are in danger of incurring the penalties which the law of God denounces against them.

Let us shortly sum up what we have endeavoured to set forth:—

1st. That the Scripture forbids all sorts of divination, or inquiring of, or by means of any creature, animate or inanimate, or of any spirit, except of God alone, concerning things secret and hidden from the natural and waking understanding and reflection of man.

2nd. That Scripture forbids the use of any means whatsoever, whereby to cause any man or spirit to give answers to such questions.

3rd. That it is a wicked thing, both in the person doing it, and in the person permitting it to be done upon them, to suspend, and *pro tempore* annihilate, a man's will and conscience, and yet give him power to act; whereby, while he does not cease, like a madman or an idiot, to be responsible, you take from him that wherein responsibility safely consists.

4th. That even where it does not open a door to acts of treachery and outrage, of which it can be proved advantage has been taken, yet that mesmerism has a permanent weakening and defiling effect on the spirits of those subjected to it.

5th. That mesmerism leads in some to divination, and divination to further spiritual wickedness in dealing with familiar spirits, and the spirits of the dead, or spirits professing to be such, and this to false doctrines of the worst and most deleterious description.

And, on the other hand, that the contemptible nature and character of the whole of the proceedings connected with the revelations made by these means, have strengthened the prevalent neology, and infidelity, and Sadducceism of the day.

Or it has, in those that believe these manifestations

to be real, led to the losing of all reverence and awe in dealing with the invisible.

But whether in all cases mesmerism leads to any of these evils or not (for many who in their ignorance have used it have been preserved by God's mercy from them), we have said enough to point out the dangers of it ; to make every one who fears God pause ; to make him shudder at the bare thought of incurring the risk, to say the least, of tampering with forbidden things, and shrink back from practising, or applying to those that practise, or subjecting himself to such 'an art ;' and to make him refuse either to put forth his hand in the use of this 'occult' power, or to be brought himself into a condition wherein he sleeps and yet is awake ; a helpless child, and yet a man to do or submit to evil ; not a dead man, nor yet a living one ; not a soul without a body, nor yet a body without a soul ; but a strange unnatural condition of both, in which the door is opened to every evil, while every power of conscience, affection, reason, memory, and will, which God has given to guard this door, is suspended and locked up in deep and deadly slumber.

Finally, we again call upon you to remember not only that it is written, 'Thou shalt not practise divination, witchcraft, ... necromancy,' &c. but also, 'Thou shalt not go to inquire of them who do such things,' nor 'seek from the living to the dead.'

And that you are equally committing sin by going to inquire of such whether they be impostors, or whether there be a reality in their acts, and in what they profess to do.

We grieve that such sins should be committed openly and unreproved in the Church and among the baptised. We grieve that such sins should be committed openly and unreproved in this our country, and fear the displeasure of God. Surely the clergy should with one voice denounce it, we say again, whether there be reality in the professors and practisers of these things, or whether they are only assuming thus to do wickedly ; and surely the Legislature should put them down with a strong hand. If there are laws against blasphemy and swearing, and against Sunday-trading, there should be laws against necromancy, and dealing with familiar spirits, even if those pretending to it were altogether impostors; still more if they are not imposing, and it be not all clever trick, but fearful reality,— and if there be a shadow of reality in it it is fearful ;— let the lawgivers and rulers of the land put down such iniquity.

Whenever these things appeared it was the sign of approaching doom,— it was the sign of a declining age, or of a declining nation. When the Canaanites practised them the measure of their iniquity was full. When Saul applied to the Witch of Endor his end was near. When these things prevailed among the Jews their day was closing. Let us not permit such amongst us, lest it should become a sign to us of declension and doom.

LONDON

PRINTED BY SPOTTISWOODE AND CO.

NEW-STREET SQUARE

Milton Keynes UK
Ingram Content Group UK Ltd.
UKHW050215070524
442290UK00008B/446

9 781535 815949